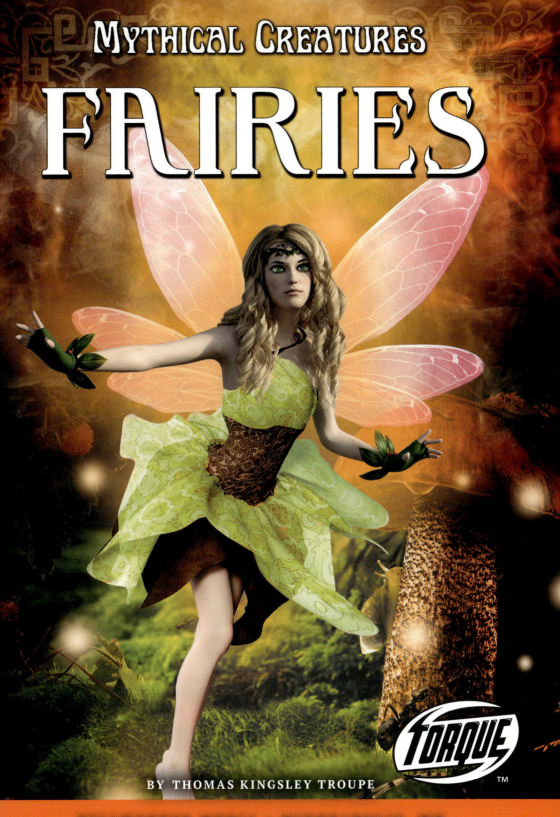

Torque brims with excitement perfect for thrill-seekers of all kinds. Discover daring survival skills, explore uncharted worlds, and marvel at mighty engines and extreme sports. In *Torque* books, anything can happen. Are you ready?

This edition first published in 2021 by Bellwether Media, Inc.

No part of this publication may be reproduced in whole or in part without written permission of the publisher.
For information regarding permission, write to Bellwether Media, Inc., Attention: Permissions Department, 6012 Blue Circle Drive, Minnetonka, MN 55343.

Library of Congress Cataloging-in-Publication Data

Names: Troupe, Thomas Kingsley, author.
Title: Fairies / by Thomas Kingsley Troupe.
Description: Minneapolis, MN : Bellwether Media Inc., [2021] | Series: Torque: Mythical creatures | Includes bibliographical references and index. | Audience: Ages 7-12 | Audience: Grades 4-6 | Summary: "Amazing images accompany engaging information about fairies. The combination of high-interest subject matter and light text is intended for students in grades 3 through 7"– Provided by publisher.
Identifiers: LCCN 2020046600 (print) | LCCN 2020046601 (ebook) | ISBN 9781644874646 | ISBN 9781648341410 (ebook)
Subjects: LCSH: Fairies–Juvenile literature.
Classification: LCC BF1552 .T725 2021 (print) | LCC BF1552 (ebook) | DDC 398.21–dc23
LC record available at https://lccn.loc.gov/2020046600
LC ebook record available at https://lccn.loc.gov/2020046601

Text copyright © 2021 by Bellwether Media, Inc. TORQUE and associated logos are trademarks and/or registered trademarks of Bellwether Media, Inc.

Editor: Rebecca Sabelko   Designer: Josh Brink

Printed in the United States of America, North Mankato, MN.

TABLE OF CONTENTS

FAIRIES IN THE TREES	4
FAIRIES AROUND THE WORLD	10
FAIRIES FOREVER!	20
GLOSSARY	22
TO LEARN MORE	23
INDEX	24

FAIRIES IN THE TREES

On a bright afternoon, you hike through a hardwood forest. Small bunnies hop across the path while birds sing. It feels like a fairy tale!

Soon you lose track of time. You turn toward home. But the trail has disappeared! Suddenly, a small fairy appears in front of you. Have you entered into the fairy **realm**?

FAIRY FLY
Woolly aphids are insects that are often called fairy flies.

Fairies are magical creatures that are often linked to nature. They usually look like tiny humans. But they can be much larger. Fairies often have wings. Some can have green hair and clothes. Others always dress in white.

Fairy **myths** are found in **cultures** all around the world. This widespread belief makes their origin unknown.

Some fairies use their magic to be **cruel**. They often play tricks. Fairies can also be dangerous. Humans who find their way into the fairy realm may be trapped there forever!

But not all fairies are nasty. Some help humans with their chores. Others help people find love. Fairies sometimes grant wishes, too!

Irish fairy doing chores

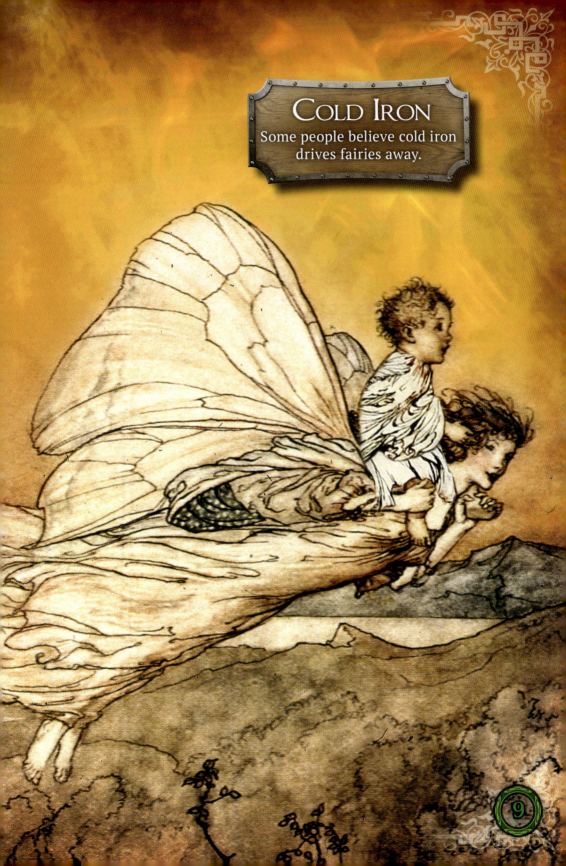

COLD IRON
Some people believe cold iron drives fairies away.

FAIRIES AROUND THE WORLD

Fairy myths have been common throughout Europe for centuries. Greek and Roman mythology included **nymphs**. These fairy-like creatures were linked to the gods.

Fairy Origins in Europe

Greece =
Rome =

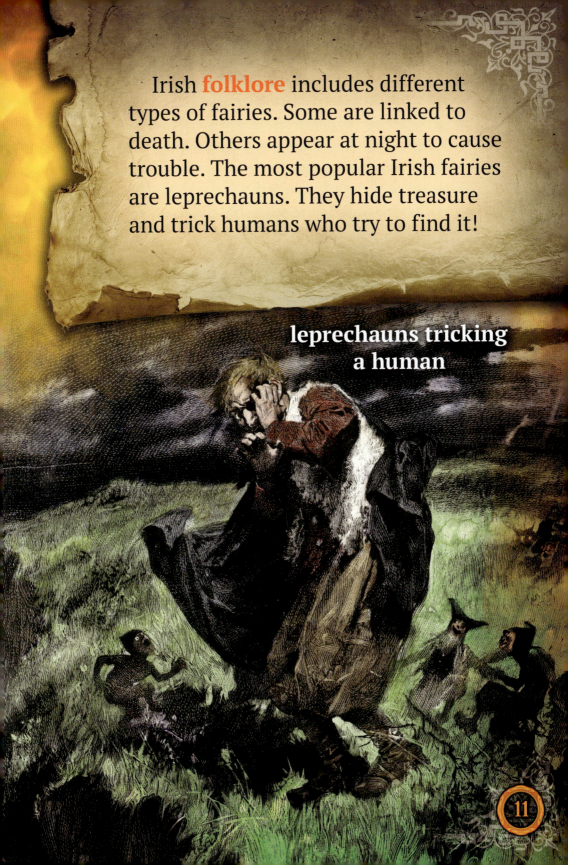

Irish **folklore** includes different types of fairies. Some are linked to death. Others appear at night to cause trouble. The most popular Irish fairies are leprechauns. They hide treasure and trick humans who try to find it!

leprechauns tricking a human

Fairies are common in Asia, too. In Vietnamese folklore, tales tell of a fairy goddess named Âu Cơ, known as the mother of the people. She loved to help people. She healed the sick.

The peri were ancient Persian fairies. They often played tricks. But they could be helpful, too. They later became kind **spirits** to some Muslims.

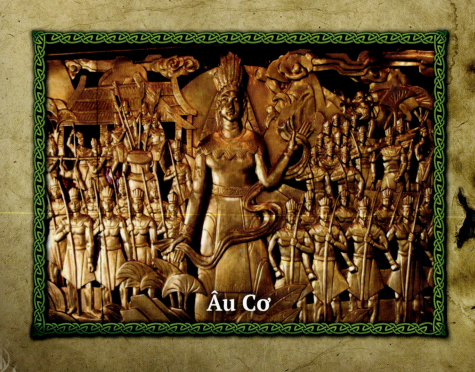

Âu Cơ

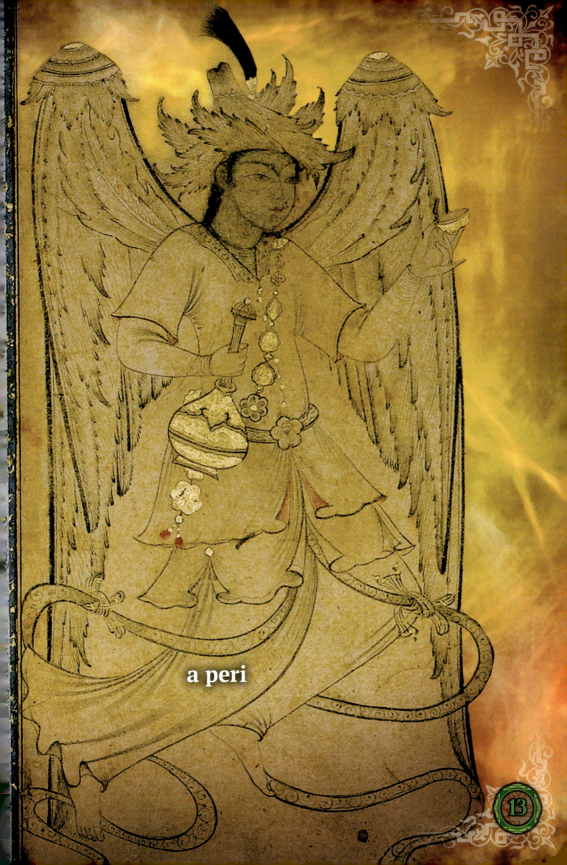
a peri

In North America, some Native American tribes share stories of "little people." These fairies can be dangerous. But many are helpful.

Jogah are Iroquois nature fairies. They protect the earth and animals. They trick humans who harm their home. But they are kind to humans who leave them gifts.

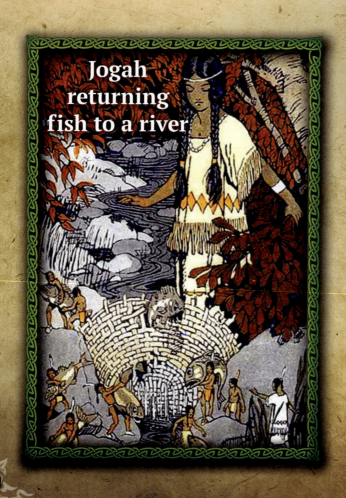

Jogah returning fish to a river

fairy godmother from *Cinderella*

Fairies began to appear in writing around the 1200s. They continued to show up in stories for hundreds of years. They took on different roles and meanings.

William Shakespeare wrote plays that featured fairy kings, queens, and **tricksters**. The French version of *Cinderella* introduced the fairy godmother. In many tales, she uses magic to help the main character.

Shakespeare's *A Midsummer Night's Dream*

Fairies became popular in **Victorian** art during the mid-1800s. Life was hard for many people in England. Fairy art helped people escape their real lives. Fairy paintings used ideas from folklore and **literature**. This allowed people to experience the stories in a new way.

Since the early 1900s, the tooth fairy has been famous in the United States. It visits children at night to collect teeth in exchange for money.

Cottingley Fairies

In 1917, two girls from England took photos with paper fairies. The photos fooled many people who thought the fairies were real. The women admitted the fairies were fake in 1983.

Fairy Timeline

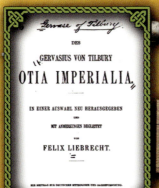

1210 to 1214: Gervase of Tilbury writes about fairies in *Otia Imperialia*

1697: The first fairy godmother appears in Charles Perrault's *Cinderella*

1927: The modern tooth fairy appears in a play written by Esther Watkins Arnold

FAIRIES FOREVER!

Fairies are still popular today. People dress as fairies for Halloween. The creatures appear in video games and films. In *The Legend of Zelda: Breath of the Wild*, fairies heal Link. Disney's famous fairy finds adventure with her friends in the *Tinker Bell* movie.

Fairies continue to **enchant** our imaginations!

Tinker Bell

Media Mention

Book Series: The Spiderwick Chronicles

Written By: Holly Black and Tony DiTerlizzi

Years Released: 2003 to 2009

Summary: A family discovers a hidden fairy world

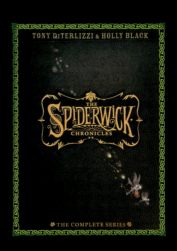

fairy Halloween costumes

GLOSSARY

cruel—wanting to cause harm

cultures—the beliefs, values, and ways of life of a group of people

enchant—to put under a magical spell

folklore—the customs, beliefs, stories, and sayings of a group of people

literature—written works, often books, that are highly respected

myths—ancient stories about the beliefs or history of a group of people; myths also try to explain events.

nymphs—fairy-like creatures that live in mountains, forests, and water

realm—an area ruled by royalty

spirits—beings whose existence cannot be explained

tricksters—fairies that play tricks on humans

Victorian—relating to the period of Queen Victoria of England's reign; the Victorian Era lasted from around 1820 to 1914.

TO LEARN MORE

AT THE LIBRARY

Lawrence, Sandra, and Stuart Hill. *The Atlas of Monsters: Mythical Creatures from Around the World.* Philadelphia, Pa.: Running Press Kids, 2019.

O'Brien, Cynthia. *Fairy Myths.* New York, N.Y.: Gareth Stevens Publishing, 2018.

Porter, Steve. *Fairies.* Minneapolis, Minn.: Bellwether Media, 2014.

ON THE WEB

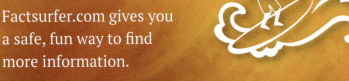

Factsurfer.com gives you a safe, fun way to find more information.

1. Go to www.factsurfer.com

2. Enter "fairies" into the search box and click.

3. Select your book cover to see a list of related content.

INDEX

appearance, 7
around the world, 15
Asia, 12
Âu Cơ, 12
Cinderella, 16, 17
Cottingley Fairies, 18
cultures, 7
Europe, 10, 11, 18
fairy godmother, 16, 17
fairy tale, 4
folklore, 11, 12, 18
Halloween, 20, 21
history, 10, 11, 12, 14, 17, 18
humans, 7, 8, 11, 14
iron, 9
Jogah, 14
Legend of Zelda, The: Breath of the Wild, 20

leprechauns, 11
literature, 18
magic, 8, 17
myths, 7, 10, 15
North America, 14, 18
nymphs, 10
origin, 7, 10
peri, 12, 13
powers, 8, 11, 12, 14, 17
realm, 4, 8
Shakespeare, William, 17
Spiderwick Chronicles, The, 21
timeline, 18-19
Tinker Bell, 20
tooth fairy, 18
tricks, 8, 11, 12, 14, 17
Victorian art, 18
woolly aphids, 4

The images in this book are reproduced through the courtesy of: Veronika Surovtseva, front cover (fairy); Valentyna Chukhlyebova, front cover (dress); Irina Kozorog, front cover (background); Atelier Sommerland, p. 3 (fairy); Teo Tarras, p. 3 (background); Jude Black, p. 4 (woolly aphid); danyssphoto, pp. 4-5 (background); Joshua Resnick, p. 5 (hiker); Science History Images/ Alamy, pp. 6-7; Chronicle/ Alamy, p. 7; Arthur Rackham/ Wiki Commons, p. 8; Charles Walker Collection/ Alamy, pp. 8-9; North Wind Picture Archives/ Alamy, p. 11; Lengoctho2207/ Wiki Commons, p. 12; Fine Art Images/ Alamy, p. 13; Csemerick/ Wiki Commons, pp. 14, 15 (top left); Album/ Alamy, p. 15 (top right); Objectum/ Alamy, p. 15 (bottom left); René Mayorga/ Wiki Commons, p. 15 (bottom right); AF Fotografie/ Alamy, pp. 16-17; Lebrecht Authors/ Alamy, p. 17; Elsie Wright/ Wiki Commons, p. 18; Carl Rumpler/ Wiki Commons, p. 19 (top); Pictorial Press/ Alamy, p. 19 (middle); Old Visuals/ Alamy, p. 19 (bottom); Art of Drawing/ Alamy, p. 20; Maja Marjanovic, p. 21; Bellwether Media, p. 21 (book); IKO-studio, p. 22 (background); Marcin Sylwia Ciesielski, p. 22 (fairy).